Ache
The Body's Experience of Religion

Flipped
Mitten
Press

Ache

The Body's Experience of Religion

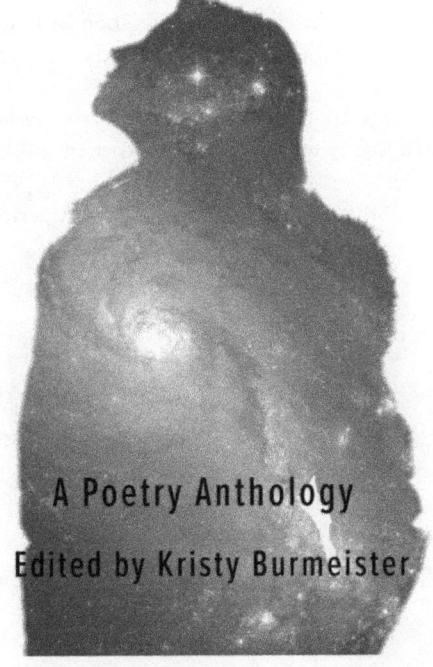

A Poetry Anthology

Edited by Kristy Burmeister

Flipped Mitten Press
703 W 2nd St, Ligonier, Indiana 46767
flippedmittenpress.com

Introduction and selection copyright © Flipped Mitten Press, LLC, 2024
All rights reserved. No part of this publication may be reproduced, distributed, or transmitted in any form or by any means, including photocopying, recording, or other electronic or mechanical methods, without the prior written permission of the publisher or author, except in the case of brief quotations embodied in critical reviews and certain other noncommercial uses permitted by copyright law.

The poems in this anthology are protected by the poet's copyright and may not be reproduced in any form without the consent of the poet.

Printed in the United States of America
First Edition, 2024

ISBN 978-0-9995700-2-9

Cover Design: Kristy Burmeister

Table of Contents

Introduction	i
Sheila Dietz, PARKING LOT PARADISE	1
David E. Poston, THE WORD	2
Alex Baskin, where god is called the Name	3
Kristin Gifford, Viriditas	4
Hera Naguib, Lessons from the Qari	6
J.J. Steinfeld, Ending Music of the Disoriented Soul	8
Bethany W. Pope, Speaking in Tongues	10
Devon Miller-Duggan, Prayer against Insomnia	12
Bernardo Villela, A(scent)	13
Holly Payne-Strange, Devotional Dinners	14
Isabel Yacura, spagyria of the liturgy	16
Neethu Krishnan, Her body as a receptacle for a Devi	18
Shannon King, Recovering Devout	19
Shannon King, Good Catholic Girl	20
Bibi B., Parika	21
Bibi B., Durand Scarf	22
Stephanie Krist, Yours No More	23
Elliot Gale, The Life Cycle of the Transsexual	24
P. Ashley Smith, blame the dress	26
Lynne Sargent, A Priestess' Carvings	28
Charisse Stephens, Transfiguration	29
Angela Martz, Prayer Circle, 1998	30
Dick Croy, PRAYER	32
Sumit Parikh, The Prayer Room	33
Allen Darwish, Canon	34
Kira Coleman, Uninvited and Without a Recommend	36
Melinda Robinson, The Flesh and the Devil	37
LaDonna Witmer, Rubies / Proverbs 31:10	38
Tara Campbell, The prophecy unswaddled	40
Tara Campbell, Vessels of the State	42
Elizabeth Johnston Ambrose, The Ten Commandments of Loving a Recovering Evangelical	44

Melanie Weldon-Soiset, Bound for Foxe's Book?	47
David Ruekberg, When God visits me	48
Trystan Popish, Pedicure	49
Madina Tuhbatullina, Tender Primates III	50
Colleen Mitchell, New Names	51
Emmie Christie, How Do I Tell You?	52
Virginia Barrett, Sunset IX [The Haight with Heaney]	53
Marie Thomas, Skin	54
Rose Menyon Heflin, The Atheist at Communion: A Sijo Sequence	56
Elizabeth Gade, Madonna Of The Morgue	57
Jane Medved, Skin Is Not Light	58
Poet Biographies	60
Acknowledgments	71

Introduction

*In what ways do we experience religion,
or the loss of religion, in our bodies?*

Religion isn't only a set of beliefs. With our bodies, we practice religion and have religion practiced upon us. As there are no barriers between soul and flesh, our bodies bear the imprint of our religious experiences.

When I asked poets to contribute to this anthology, I wanted to explore the many experiences we have within our varied bodies and within our varied religious communities.

The poems in this collection explore the beauty and pain found in these physical experiences of religion. Some poems are nostalgic, evoking an aching sense of longing for a simpler time and simpler faith. Others speak to the connection between physical sensations and the experience of the divine. Many of them describe the embodied experience of a person without institutional power within a religion.

I'm grateful to each poet who participated in this anthology. While each poem reflects one individual person's bodily experience and could stand on its own, when read collectively, each poet's voice is amplified by the others. In reading this anthology, I hope you can slip into each poet's shoes for a moment and better understand the wide range of experiences humans can have within our religious traditions.

~ Kristy Burmeister, *editor*

Sheila Dietz

Parking Lot Paradise

We park beside a muddy truck.
My eyes open slowly to a chilly drizzle.
Rest stop parking lot: 95 North,
time for a break, coffee,
maybe an egg and cheese.

Across the thin strip of grass, a man,
facing his car door, shawl draped over his head,
bows repeatedly. But something more stirs
the air around him—a rhythm,
purposeful, spirited. A companion,
his long side locks twisted and curled,
hurries through the rain carrying
drinks in paper cups, hops in the car
while his friend swirls his hands in the air
as if to waft his prayer, sending raindrops
splattering into each other.

A girl, about 11, comes running down the sidewalk,
a younger boy close behind. They wear T-shirts
and shorts in the rain, heavier now, and seem suddenly
to be moving in slow motion, rippling
reflected clouds as they splash through puddles,
laughing and I believe I can see each drop
bounce off the boy's pumping arms,
the girl's knees as they pass us
backing out of our spot.
They seem like angels.
I want them to be angels.

David E. Poston

The Word

"And the Word was made flesh, and dwelt among us, and we beheld his glory..." John 1:14

Still small enough to lie on my back
under the sea of lay folk gathered
in the charged heat of that Kentucky night,
I nestled my head in Mother's lap,
my eyes swimming after black dots
that rode the currents of the sanctuary's murky heights
to swoop and batter themselves into pale globes
hanging from chains with rusty links,

until the sudden hush brought me back,
and I first heard His name
muttered, then sighed, then thundered:

Jesus, Jesus, o sweet Jesus.

Mighty waters, looming wall,
bodies surging all around me,
arms upraised in swells of adoration.

Then, it was I, six summers later,
doing a spindly dance in the surf on Ocean Isle,
singing *Lord, lift me up on higher ground!*
in some wild, full-throttled key, in my boy-king joy
not caring I was lost
in rolling andantinos of green water
lifting me, not knowing as I felt that glory
swell through me once again
how I would miss it when it ebbed away.

Alex Baskin
where god is called the Name

during torah reading, we played lion king/
zig-zagging in the coat room, we were cave hyenas
swaddled, draped, enveloped in found layers/
in spring, it was handball in the parking lot/

there were dark glass doors
but familiar suits shuffled in through the side/
the ceiling was low, not high/
the shul's carpet was green and worn/

always late, my father would smirk—
you know, aleinu is really the most important part anyway/

after davening they served entenmann's donuts/
loud men poured whiskey at 11am/

once I hugged a skirt-leg and looked up and it was not my mother/
fear drizzled/my body sometimes shaky/I was never lost/

I couldn't and still can't pronounce pentateuch
but it blew my mind that one book can be called so many different things/

on yom kippur, bonds are sold for a dream too-realized/
all across the calendar, prayers beg salvation for some/

when I asked my mother to stop waking me up on saturdays
she cried, afraid she would lose me/

a question mark lodged in my throat/
one foot in, one foot out/
then repenting, atoning
insisting that I'll put all three of my feet in/

Kristin Gifford

Viriditas

For Jon

> *Medieval nun, scientist, theologian and composer, Hildegard Von Bingen, created the word "viriditas" for the greening power of the divine that pulsates through all things.*

Raised knee-deep in original sin, fed
the blood of Christ from small plastic cups
each Sunday, my prayers unspooled
each night into the dark of my bedroom,
desperate to snag Jesus back in my heart.
But always the talk of that which cannot
be forgiven and hell, forever hell, waiting
with its sure finality, doors flung wide
and eager. On the cross, the shriveled candle
of Christ's body dripped sweat. I swung
my feet below the wooden pew to stay awake,
to keep from falling further from grace.
In partitioned rooms below the sanctuary,
children killed giants with stones
and righteous floods wiped all life from earth
in shocks of judgment. Kings held swords
to heads of infants and fathers tied children
on stacks of wood, lifted glinting blades above
their stretched necks. *The B-I-B-L-E*
we sang full throated as the old piano staggered
along and God nodded his grim approval.
I kissed my first boy in that basement.

Heard the word period and knew Kelsey
got hers first. Had my training bra snapped
by a boy who, later, on our missions' trip
to Minneapolis would sit with me, staring
out blood-stained glass in the Basilica,
and ask if God was real before getting drunk
and killing himself in a crash. Jon, the boy
with dimples and dark hair, who came up
with me from Ms. Mahoney's Kindergarten
class. Jon, speeding wildly, far from doctrine,
soaring under attentive stars, over the hushed
green hearts of Iowa beans, into the soft arms of fire.

Hera Naguib
Lessons from the Qari

On nights slammed in sweat,
as on my thirteenth summer,
what still haunts: hellfire the qari
warned of & the strapped heels,
the flaming braids for my white
lies, Mondays I squandered
to Rick Dees Top 40s, death-wish
I hurled my head for in buckets
of water, & each look the boy and I
scalloped from the backseat
of the school bus & across
alleyways as the Jeddah heat
flexed in the rose finch's gullet,
the meadow-saffron screeched
a frill, & the qari, dim echo
in mind, admonished—
the first glance at man is an accident,
the second glance is forbidden.
But how quickly a girl
cottons to her own
concealment—evenings I'd spill
an abaya over a pale kameez
hugged at the midriff,

heady with nicotine,
and the chuka chuka
chuk warmth of needles
punching holes in the moist
cavity of a tailor shop.
How quickly a girl learns
only the inanimate will cede
to passion, like the feckless dark
I would meet him in,
of empty houses shaded by
the touch-me-nots;
the discarded tables and cots
intuiting our limbs,
both Muslim,
both teenage and urging—

J. J. Steinfeld

Ending Music of the Disoriented Soul

Falling through memory and history
mind and body caught in a concert of existence
an absurd recounting, standing/falling room only
the disoriented soul hears a siren song off-key
upstaged by the *Song of Songs* grumbled forth
then a succession of singsong accusations
against eternity, against the end of the world
against its chaotic beginnings, against endings
a medley of recriminations

no, this cannot be, this cannot be
the disoriented soul shouts as if melodic words
can become a song of rescue or escape

how the mind and body respond
when the finale looms
like sudden music from nowhere
and everywhere, lyrics unending
the contradictions beautiful cacophony

hymns of the past, chants to the future,
catchy and lively tunes from a lifetime
entire symphonies misplaced by chronology
compositions sacred, compositions profane
compositions unsure of the sacred or the profane
seconds become entangled in forever
a love song long-ago heard on a vanished radio
forever becomes a second, a song from childhood
a mother's unforgotten lullaby

then the disoriented soul
begins to sing a song
to finish the descent
the concert of existence
concluded with only
the slightest applause.

Bethany W. Pope
Speaking in Tongues

An icon of cheap, brittle plastic
(the texture of a necco wafer)
was pressed into the wet sand of the road.
The pink back, sun-faded and piebald,
caught under the toe of my boot,
snagging me like the time (breaking
into an abandoned house) I misstepped and shot
a three inch nail through my sole. It emerged
through the top, gleaming wetly, with malevolence,
and I hid it from my parents for a week.
I hid it until my sister eventually noticed the smell.
If Christ was pinned to the cross
with a red-iron spike, it would have
been driven in above the ankles.
Anywhere else and the flesh would tear
like a licorice whip, unraveling
from the bone in slick, bright ropes.
Anyway, this was a different kind of icon.
When I flipped over the arched token,
paper Guanyin stared up at me, throned,
and garlanded, pointing towards her chest,
and I was back in Sacred Heart,
sneaking into the rear of the sanctuary
in the middle of the service, with my dog
and my guilty protestantism, fingering
the bakelite beads of the rosaries that dangled
in the shop, like vines, and wondering
how the fuck, exactly, they were supposed to work.
The church was in the Spanish style
(pink tiles, flat roof, a plain, peach spire)
and a garden filled with the kind of rancorous,

untamable vegetation that does well in the heat.
There was a fountain filled with chlorinated water,
bluer than the Virgin's veil, with a gray statue
of Mary standing in it with her arms spread.
Surely goodness and mercy will follow me,
all the days of my life, but I never expected mercy
to show up looking like this. I slipped Guanyin
into my pocket, next to a bead,
a stone, between my keys, and my flesh,
yanked back like a dog on a chain
to something I longed for then, and long for still,
but have never been able to reach.

Devon Miller-Duggan

Prayer against Insomnia

I remember air and light more singingly than words and faces.
recall tastes more than scents, have come to believe
ceasing to wish harm drags me as close to forgiveness as
the void in me, around me, ever will permit.

Night shuts down my ability to close thousand voices and too-bright
colors of the day. These days, some county of this body
chokes itself into bruise or screech, white-hot spikes,
reliable dull aches. Having, holding a body means

dying of every kind of thirst for some remembered water.
Remembered light (salt light & balsam, dust-refracted sun & pinyon-sage)
paints itself into the throat of sleeplessness.
Red dream pushes itself across the void-that-screams into a bridge. Please
fly.

Bernardo Villela

A(scent)

Closed eyes
soul exposed
old woody-
scented pews.

Barely breathing
must invades the
olfactory
as must must.

Focus comes
with divine
assistance.

With a scent
comes ascent
soul uplifted
crescent
     inner-light
         that radiates
             into momentary transcendence.
Peace.   Bliss.

All begun
with the invasion
of sense memory.
        The exalting odor
        that hearkens to
simpler times
        and
            deeper faith
    returning anew
    to gift me
    strength.

Holly Payne-Strange
Devotional Dinners

Wednesdays are my favorite.
The kitchen alive with
Hissing pans and half baked bread
With rosemary fresh from the garden
And the pop of a cork,
Red wine splashing into a glass.
Simple things.
But together, a mosaic,
Each a tessera of vivid, startling pleasure.

She takes my hands
Washing them with water gathered from the Agean.
Our entranceway to the sacred.
I do the same for her,
Droplets on her knuckles
Like a vanishing fresco.
And suddenly,
I want to dance.

From that point on
Everything
Is magic.

The oven has become a hearth for Hestia,
The herbs a blessing from Demeter,
The music a gift from Dionysus.

And all of it woven together
By the two Hellenists
Playing at a loom,
Almost lost
To time.

And so we eat, play, talk,
Reveling in our senses,
Like a treasure trove.
Reconstructing
Ancient joy.

Each bite, each step, each sniff
A glorious, sensual reminder
Of what our bodies can do.
And how much we have
To vividly experience.

Before the night must end.

The things get put away
And we return to a
Normal
Mundane
Rhythm.
But we always know.
The magic will come
Back.

Isabel Yacura
spagyria of the liturgy

To lay the imagined thumb on the mouth, there in the hazy dark, opening only to the silent room.
Chrismus, nominative.
Chrismum, accusative.
Chrisme, vocative—
E-vocative, perhaps, a tasteless electric segue into something holy, something unknown, something of a child searching for lower-case god in the charcoal of half-drunk sleep.
A thing of failed chrysopoeia, the base metals of myself dull and reductive, landing forever back on faith i had no hand in nor real belief—an easy shorthand for what i imagine must be—
the hand—my hand, at long last, recognizable only in the way my fingertips are longing for it, twitching, my hand remembering—tangles in the sheets —the back of the shirt.
The spirit being flesh/blood/heat, under my grasping hands. Accusatory and indicative and named, for once. Six cases, seventh vestigial or vestal— swearing myself again to the sacred hearth. Pretending that i can regrow virginity, or at least make myself a ship, every seven years a new thing.
The prima materia as a lifeline that cuts into my fingers, rubedo re-entry. Sacrament. Like i said.
Fumbling for excuses with a thick stupid tongue—this dull piece of muscle, this thing that aches, this lossless desperation for transmutation—
The willing lamb, shochet-slaughtered, outside this long purview of false catholicism. To be said, then:

"As in the Latin term, then, sacrifices of all kinds are linked with an approach to divinity."

Accusatory, again, always, never-escaping, that i would be so martyred and still open my mouth for communion.

Paeniteō—2. To regret, repent, to be sorry.

Conjugated into the future active participle **paenitūrus** (*feminine* **paenitūra**)—

About to regret. About to be sorry.

The act of bended knee comes easier with the reality of the hand at the back of the neck. Rattled, dumped clean like an etch-a-sketch—i avert my eyes. Myself as an anchoress whose walls have been unlaid by the same who mixed the mortar. A failed transubstantiation, a smoking ruin of what should've been the stone.

No states and no princes, no sun rising.

Neethu Krishnan

Her body as a receptacle for a Devi

Ruby eyes, inky lips, amethyst cheeks,
Fluent in vile hands and throaty laughs,
She still startles sometimes at
Draupadi-lauding mouths,
Saraswati-worshipping hands.
Where day is night, existence consent,
Stiletto tips, tasers, tactical knives
Are but inconspicuous covers
For the sword, the trident, the mace
She and her sisters carry within,
Because supposedly, mythically, scripturally,
Her body is also the abode of a Devi,
Though apparently not one of her choosing,
For she has only ever known
An unfortunate, patriarchally palatable,
Survival-necessitated farce, where
She is — has to be — only ever
The armoured defensive, never
The revered divine.

Shannon King

Recovering Devout

you can stop
being catholic,
but the guilt
lingers for
2000 more years

signed paperwork
in Sunday school,
at 12 years old
that I would
wait for marriage

you are a cupcake,
everytime someone
takes a lick, you
become more
and more
worthless
--- Sunday school
teacher told me so

I forgot her name
and face but I
recall how her
husband dying in
9/11 brought her
closer to God

--- Is that a God
worth forgiving?

Shannon King
Good Catholic Girl

baptized
screaming drowning
leathery priest without
gentle hands

baby knows its mother
is no virgin mary
9 months
haunted womb shared with
dead sperm of many

first communion
bread stale,
dry
wine cheap
no flavourful hints of citrus
only misguidance

the most revered woman in the church:
her vagina, hymen intact
inspirational

mom, you raised me
your good catholic daughter

every time you masturbate,
God kills a puppy
i alone
emptied the SPCA

Bibi B.
Parika

I have visions of writing scripture in menstrual blood
my nails grow and wind inward like goat's horns
hair sprouting from every pore in my body
cascading down like a black silk burka
in my dreams my spine cracks
ribs flare outward like scraped-velvet wings
jewels and flowers fall from my lips
as I recite in reverse
offering my throbbing liver to the
battalion men; swords drawn codpieces polished
trying to pour lead in my mouth
while they gather lapis and tulips off the soil
counting their loot before stoning the blasphemer

I have been raised on heroes and demons
only the demons have bodies like mine

Bibi B.
Durand Scarf

rag-head, don't you know
    I don't like the way
you've bound yourself up
    these white men carve me up
succumbed to the pressures
    with their eyes and their smiles
of your savage culture
    like they're processing meat
and weak, docile nature
    scoring border lines on the dermal map
you don't need to do that here
    ripping apart breast and rump and thigh
you can put your skin on proud display
    so I wrap myself up for safekeeping
and no man can ever take
    free from my body at last
that freedom away from you

Stephanie Krist
Yours No More

My body was not truly mine
from 17-29.

My depression promised (never enough)
My religion preached (a temple)
My fertility decided (miscarriage)

Those who should have loved me
no matter what (size) threw
'concerns' shaped like judgements
at shapes that naturally changed.

I spent years reclaiming
my own self, my own heart,
starting with more tattoos,
more food, more celebration,
less mileage, less hiding,
less expectation.

Pr(a)ying eyes have no hold
on me, I am free.

My body is yours no more.

Elliot Gale
The Life Cycle of the Transsexual

the Creator
punishes His sandchild
for the sake of its nature; dogwhipped
for its ache to Be; how
could we defend the Hand
that does commit such an Act? shall we
condemn the fire for its dare to singe? o God,

this, this is a new coating of Hell.

the sand,
       it crawls
              walks
                     stoops
it hopes and it prays to a god whose head floats in the clouds
    amen, amen,
it gasps for breath after it falls back to earth
it peels and it laments
it howls at the Sun
it burns under the Moon
it prays to Hell to take it away
it prays to God, *please, do me a kindness*
    and let me choke on Thy Blood
    just a little quicker; show me
    Thy Mercy and i will no longer
    ooze Bile into ratty carpet, where
    it will retain my sins in an endless
    installation, on view now and open to the public, and the
    Bleach punched into it— nothing—
    for God's righteous sake, take me into Thy Arms!

the Creator does not hear.

the sand washes itself in the river
gritskin clean, wrapped in the wrong linen
it tumbles down cliffs, grassitch hills,
into smoggy sea and swaying hunchback limbs
pushed lower and lower,
all bruised by the Creator's hand

this, this coating of Hell is nothing new.

P. Ashley Smith

blame the dress

of all the dresses on the rack you select the most modest
        buttoned up hem to neck in virginal pearls

the dark fabric (feminine & ditsy) a tame floral
        chosen not to attract attention

you have always hidden in secondhand rejects
        church ladies' sagging gifts pulled from trash bags

this is the first time you get to pick from the juniors section
        the dress is not your favorite but it will appease

you know your wants (bright colors; flash of skin) are sin
        but oh! to wear a size not sizes too large

you have eaten from the tree of good and evil
        wandered the department store of temptation

forced pearls through slits into submission
        now you know the seductive call of a perfect fit

on the edge of childhood
        about to dive into the waters of desire and being desired

you are a good girl   you know beauty is a forbidden fruit
        it trips up the beholder   sends them stumbling

your self must control how you are seen
        how others react to the seeing

you are a good girl   you will carry this responsibility
          in silence without shoulder pads

on the linoleum catwalk you are young
          a girl in a new frock   feeling pretty

the tips of your knees wink out
          you pirouette for approval & stumble

over the words
                    no
return it
          you make me think thoughts

no father should have
          about his daughter

you are a girl modestly dressed
          arousing attention   fermenting shame

for years you will blame the girl
          &   blame the dress

Lynne Sargent

A Priestess' Carvings

I have forgotten my skin
free of swords, unadorned
by even the stabs I gave myself,
that I might be first
to claim my flesh's blood,
carved like careful runes
for rituals

and now I am naked,
unprimed

and will have to struggle through
nonetheless, play shaman, priestess
to a forgotten temple, covered
in vines,

but I will make it vital again,
water it with new wounds
decorate its belly with scars
excavate crystals, trace
careful circles and stars,

and some day
the new moon will come again
and my skin, and all its markings
will glow silver in her light.

Charisse Stephens
Transfiguration

I am this:

a body
that talks to itself.

I am the way
I talk to myself;
I am my own
voice and the words
it speaks.

I am the voice of my god:
I am the voice
that I thought was the mind-
voice of God;

I was the voice
that told myself
my hopelessness
was neither final
nor failure.

I am that voice
that has been all this time
on my own side:

I am my own body;
I am the dream of my body;
I am the body

of my dream.

Angela Martz
Prayer Circle, 1998

His callused mechanic's fingers
gently hold my right hand while
the high school jazz saxophonist squeezes my left—

Tightly.

Heads bow in reverence to an unseen Lord.

He speaks
and the Spirit is drawn to him

into him

through him.

He's our righteous mentor,
holy lightning rod,
charging this closed circuit.

My hand warms as energy
spreads from him,
up my wrist,
my arm,
into my entire body.

I don't pray out loud.
I rarely do.

But I push the energy I'm receiving out of myself,
into the saxophonist,
giving him as much as he needs.

I'm a fuse,
never keeping this divine current for myself,
(because that would be selfish)
but allowing it to pass through me.

Through us.

The prayer ends.

Hands let go,
but our fingers still tingle
as we drift off to our own corners.

We smile because we think we're grounded.
We don't know the electric storm is on the way.

I don't know a fuse can crack.

Dick Croy

Prayer

When desire and gratitude
   converge in prayer
When perceived need
emptiness behind the
   thing wished for
becomes an overflowing joy
in one's mere existence
Then is time eclipsed
   by the moment
The world by the human heart
Wanting and having
Wanter and wanted
All expressions of the
   soul's longing
Are restored in prayer
To reverence for what is
   and is not.

Sumit Parikh

The Prayer Room

My dada loved all the splendor of the Indian gods -
his rituals with pint-sized deities in the doll-house temple
in his apartment in the sky in Vile Parle, Mumbai

Dressing up his heroes in saffron robes
delicate bracelets set in pearls of rose
garlands of gold and gems

fresh rusty marigolds each morning
a diva to light each night
many many many chants each day

followed by a sleeve
of hand-rolled cigarettes
and a cask of Chivas
in an air-tight air-conditioned room

We'd speak very quietly,
after prayer time
at breakfast
or lunch
& dinner

Else we might get pulled
into his sealed room
that had the lights
turned off

Where the lock would click
and I was held
till his hand tired
or I quieted

I also prayed a lot

My dada died young

Dada – grandfather
Diva – a small open oil lamp used at prayer time

Allen Darwish

Canon

I crash erasers back behind the school,
The chalk dust booming out, a choking cloud,
A punishment for breaking some small rule,
Alone, away from all the noisy crowd

I hear at recess playing in the snow,
With sleds, and castles, shrieking in delight.
They do not understand, they cannot know:
I'm happy in this corner, lone and white,

Where other boys can't mock my every sore,
My weight, my breathing, or my faded ties,
And where the priests and teachers can't ignore
The kickings, and the beatings, and my cries.

Back in the building, that's where it's not safe,
Where God is love, unless your desk is messed,
Where Christ is merciful, but stern rules chafe,
And where the Church is Mother, for the blessed-

But I was never blessed, and ever wrong.
I learned beatitudes and knew the truth:
God's Kingdom shall be given to the strong,
God's love shall pierce the weak with nail and tooth.

In spirit, I was broken, deep inside;
In flesh, I hid my bruises, 'neath my clothes.
In mind, I dreamed of flight, my tears all dried,
My mended self held safe, in warm repose-

Oh, shattered little second-grader fool!
Escape was not my fate; no, four more years
Where worship had become a spiteful tool
And sacraments the engine of my fears.

For worse was still to come: great visions rammed
Into our little heads, repeatedly,

The endless, burning torment of the damned,
In black details, our teachers spoke with glee.

And endless, burning nightmares in the dark
Kept me from sleep for years, and haunt me still.
Sometimes I still wake sweating, feel the mark
Of Satan's touch upon my soul grown chill,

Grown bitter, fearful, guilty; Catholic kid
Still in the Church, though oft I wonder why,
For all the times I ran away and hid
Among the pews, down on the floor; I'd cry

And beg the Lord deliver me from sin,
For this was all my fault, that much was plain.
Yet still I hoped that healing might begin
And wash me clean with gentle, perfect rain.

And healing came, but decades from the boy
Who wept himself to sleep in fear of death;
And yet, the man knows Faith can still destroy
And crush the soul and heart with every breath.

And on that day, when I suffered,
Broken down in mind and spirit,
Alone in a hallowed place, I knew:
This is my body,
Given up for no one.
This is my blood,
Of no important covenant,
Shed for no one.
And my sins will be eternal;
They shall be the only memory of me.
Amen.

Kira Coleman

Uninvited and Without a Recommend

They told me my body was a temple, that it belonged to God, that He was kindly allowing me to use it for my time on Earth, but they never told me what they do if somebody enters the temple uninvited, and without a recommend.

I didn't have a temple recommend when I applied to transfer to BYU, walked into the bishop's office at my previously scheduled time, and answered a list of questions for my ecclesiastical endorsement. The bishop insisted now was a good time to get one, asked me another set of questions that I was not prepared for.

"I've never had sex that — well I've never had sex that was — the fact that there was sex was not the most screwed up thing about this situation," I explained. I hadn't yet learned that we don't call it breathing swimming and not breathing swimming — we call it swimming and drowning.

"I would encourage you to repent and become worthy of a temple recommend," he said. I guess he hadn't yet learned that we don't apologize for the things that were done to us, or that telling a woman to repent for having been raped is no way to lead her down the path of God, or that we don't have to rededicate a temple if somebody enters uninvited and without a recommend.

Melinda Robinson
The Flesh and the Devil

Never quite got the hang
Of how I was supposed to love my body
Made in the image and likeness of an incarnate deity
– a microcosm, obviously incomplete
Lacking that all important member that would allow
Divine potency to flow through my spirit
To transmute base, man-made substances
Into divinity, soul, flesh, blood –
To love, as I said, my body,
The vessel into which life was poured
And where the substance of man,
His base desires,
Were transmuted into blood, flesh, soul
And the likeness of divinity.
This body with its hidden inner temple
That I held inviolate until the veil of flesh was torn
The empty sanctum where the holy of holies remained bereft
Until the conquering potency stormed in
To perform that sacred work
For which only man can be ordained,
The work that wrested from me the right to my own life
And filled the tabernacle with his flesh and blood.
And like I said, I never understood
How I was supposed to love this body
While making war
Against the flesh of which it's made.

LaDonna Witmer
Rubies / Proverbs 31:10

You'll make a good wife.
A mother. A Christian
school teacher.

You can marry a preacher.
A missionary. A Christian
school principal.

You need no adornment
other than virtue. Charm
is deceitful and beauty
is vain.

A woman who fears the Lord
shall be praised.

Your desire shall be
for your husband, and he
shall rule over you.

For Adam came first
then Eve from his ribcage.
And it was she who fell
for the snake.

So you will exercise no authority.
He is the head of the house.
Be subject. Submissive. Ask
for permission to speak.

Devote yourself to good
(womanly) work with
willing hands and a
cheerful heart. Wash
the feet of the saints.
Care for the afflicted.
Throw (non-alcoholic)
dinner parties.

Be gentle. Be chaste.
Be a keeper at home.
Bear the children and
bring them up, too.
Put dinner on the table
no later than six.

You have childbearing hips
that will work out well. And oh
your fine nipples! The very shape
for suckling small ones. But for
Christ's sake, cover them.
We'll have no Jezebels here.

An excellent wife who can find?
Her price is far above rubies.

Tara Campbell
The prophecy unswaddled

Disregard, if it distresses you, the churn
of bodies, slap of flesh
on tile. Ignore the bend
of knee, the twist of hip. Swaddle
your senses in believers' fire:
you are the vessel

that will bear the vessel
of the vessel that will churn
out the vessel of our Lord. The fire
that shimmies inside your flesh
is merely the desire to swaddle
up our future vessel and bend

your arms around her. Around every bend
you'll imagine fresh threats to your vessel,
causing you to pull her swaddle
tighter—a danger in itself. Your mind will churn
with each disaster that could befall her flesh,
every drop her drowning, every spark the fire

that could burn her alive. But fire
is necessary. If that distresses you, try to bend
your mind toward joy. Find it in the flesh
that led you here, secure in your path as vessel.
Surely you can find comfort in the churn
of your fellows, the bodies that swaddle

you whole. Won't you swaddle
them with your limbs in turn, return the fire
that burns in them for you, the churn

of hips, fingertips grazing the bend
of your knee, slipping from thigh to vessel,
gripping anointed flesh?

Not everyone is blessed with holy flesh.
Precious few have been chosen to swaddle
the vessel of the future vessel's vessel
of our Lord. Don't you want to feel the fire
of fellowship inside you, every bend
of your body enveloped in this glorious churn?

Where are you going, vessel? Who granted you your own flesh?
How dare you reject the churn of prophesy, a Lord to swaddle?
Who let you glimpse the fire of your soul, impossible to bend?

Tara Campbell

Vessels of the State

we
will no longer
refuse you

we
will give birth
and give birth
to all required infants
from all of our partners
and all our assailants
and we will give birth
to whatever we can
from babies
to manna
to bibles
to frying pans
we will give birth
to world peace and war
we will give birth
to more
and more
and more

and we will give birth
to swarms of locusts
and shaggy red devils
with razor-sharp horns
and we will give birth
to dashing steel daggers
and gleaming new teeth
and we will give birth
to braziers and pitchforks
to praise you

for you we will grow
as many vaginas
as Kali has arms
our vulvas will steam
sulfuric, primordial,
deliver your mandates
and scald doctors' hands
with vesuvial pitch

we'll never stop birthing
and crossing state lines
dropping your children
like land mines
until tempests whirl
from sin-tainted chasms
and chains pour forth
from between our legs
to hold us down
and still
we will bear lava
and wait for our lovers
our husbands
our rapists
our fathers
our uncles
our brothers
we'll bear for them too
and praise them
and raise up new sons
and new vessels
just as you command of us
vessels of the state

Elizabeth Johnston Ambrose

The Ten Commandments of Loving a Recovering Evangelical

1. Don't mistake her as easy.
   She's spent her life on her knees
   slaking her thirst, thimble by thimble.
   Her degenerate mouth is dry of divine.
   Which means you'll do.

2. Don't try to compete
   with her alpha O mega flesh-
   made-word-made-flesh again.
   A little death's a little death and, anyway,
   He'll always talk a better game.
   He's been wooing her since the womb

3. which you should understand
   she's still trying to understand

   as/is
   part/all
   of/ her

   but

   always/never/should be

   &

   never/definitely/in certain cases

   yours

4.   which is also to say, before you undress her
acknowledge her Daddy
issues are no joke
> *(A God, a Son, and a Holy Spirit*
> *walk into a bar and ask for a Virgin Mary.*
> *The bartender says:*
> *Get a womb.)*

5.   Take seriously her wicked
sense of humor, whittled while waiting
on the receiving end of the Good
Word's punch
line. And because she's spent
an eternity waiting to be
plucked

6.   she's going to be all kinds
of mixed up about your rose petal
candlelit bubble bath fantasy
(how long in that tub
how long drowning).

7.   You'll have to learn
to speak in tongues, carnal
communion she's (c)literally craving
since that sunrise service when she hurled
her hysteric hymn-sung hymn-singed
self into the aisle, hollow hollering
entermesavemeannihilatemeremakeme

        baby o baby o baby
        because it's all about the milk & honey,
        honey.

8.   Now steel yourself. The taste
        of iron sharpens iron
        and hers is the strength
        of stonings.

9.   And if her three-bourbons-in-fire
        -and-brimstone-filled-to-the-brim-
        kind-of-crazy-cunning-lingual
        love scares you,
        make no idol threats.

10.   I told you already:
        One distant deity is as good as another.

        This was never about you.

Melanie Weldon-Soiset
Bound for Foxe's Book?

Someone wants to be a martyr,
to have golden egg tempera shine
behind her head, to gain
hagiographic status. Someone wants
to clutch the weapon of her death
in one hand, and a symbol of the faith in another.
Perhaps her left hand will hold
a prophetic book, and her right hand
a blazing iron rack,
so that catechumens can wonder,

what was she thinking?
What she's thinking right now:
she wants someone else to lead
the workout at the gym. That's it.
She can't remember if she should
jab or uppercut first. In her exhaustion,
she just bobs and weaves.
Someone picks up a book, and wonders,
who wrote it? Someone else?

David Ruekberg
When God visits me

When God visits me He appears at first as a smell
of citrus in my wife's hair

and the next morning as a certain oppressive
yet beautiful humidity after the 3 a.m. thunderstorm.

The day after that, I'm lying on the couch
when He emerges from my belly-button

reminding me of the old days
when I swam in the green light beneath my mother's navel

and anticipated life like a birthday
instead of a sentence that grows more predictable as it nears
    its conclusion.

God waves all that aside with a gesture
of layered clouds viewed from a hammock

at eight p.m. on a night in June.
"There, there," He coos, as His hand moves in slow circles

over that particular place on my back
that lets me know I am loved.

Trystan Popish

Pedicure

from the Latin pes, ped- *"foot"* + curare *"to attend to"*

I pick a purple polish. On my toes,
it looks like blood—not red like you'd assume
but deep like Homer's wine-dark sea—a shade
I christen for myself "The Blood of Christ."
For weeks I can't stop staring at my feet,
expecting toes to pulse and nails to gush
hot, frothy blood that's not my own, but proof
of years of sipping from communion's cup.

Once, Mary Magdalene washed Jesus' feet
with tears. I've not cried for him for years,
nor have I thought about his feet pierced through.
Christ, I thought that I was over you.
So tell me: why am I tormented by
my own damned, bloody nails?

Madina Tuhbatullina
Tender Primates III

I burnt my face on the side of the mountain,
rosed my cheek on red rocks. Do I surrender
in your fantasy? Look up and open palms?
This sand is not my sand,
I am a false dune.

How many deaths brought the mountain to my cheek?

I shed a little dust every day,
pay the flies. We digest each other.
we can't look upward anymore,
too sentient for innocence.

Colleen Mitchell

New Names

If your name should be honey on my lips
Why does it bloody my tongue to speak
It these days?
You are Sky Dweller and Shape Shifter,
Midwife and Mountaintop.
You said you would give me a new name
but I have reversed the invitation.
Does it wound your Spirit
When I call myself Truth Teller?
The glass in my throat has shattered
And I have spit out the shards.
I'm licking my lips
And the air is filled with the scent of apples.
I don't know whether this is freedom or the fall
But either way I like the taste of it.

Emmie Christie
How Do I Tell You?

How do I tell you I no longer lift my hands
Or grind my knees down to the guilt?
I've built my gilded edges up from the hard work
Of speaking to my inner child.
She does not want to let you go.

You would say, "You did not try hard enough,
You were never close as you claimed,
You must have faked the shakes, the tears,
The sense of cosmic blessing."

You would say this with a barrier in your eyes,
For if you concede my reality,
You would have to rethink yours.
I must let you go.

How do I tell you I find comfort in the space,
In the emptiness from your weighted words?
I study the stars and find solace in their science
Instead of forcing them to find kings for me.

How do I tell you how I see you, now,
Cowering in the same cave you were born in
And where you raised me?
How do I tell you about the sky singing of logic
And self-worth? You would weep for my wandering,
Proclaim I will die in the wild.

So, I let you go.
I do not know how to tell you I am happy.

Virginia Barrett

Sunset IX
[The Haight with Heaney]

Small round clouds collected over
the park hold the last of sun—tall

eucalyptus in sight. Just this morning
I read his poem about how St. Kevin, lost

in prayer, found a bird had built her nest
in his upturned palm, thrust through

the bars of his narrow cell. He didn't rise
from his knees until the eggs were "hatched

and fledged and flown." No patience
of a saint, but the need in me to stand

quite still on the street corner looking
up, arms by my side aching to rise

but for cars going by—how I would appear
weird to people eager to get home before

dark, so early now. Orison to fleeting
color in a shifting sky, "forgotten self,

forgotten bird," the night-praise coming.

Marie Thomas

Skin

I don't remember the first time I ate my skin.
But I remember when I first dug my nails under the whitened edges. My feet were small and I liked the satisfaction of digging and peeling it.

When I first attacked my hands, my feet had grown larger.
It was during the days we went to Mass, Mass for days and days for years. I'd sit, waiting to consume the Flesh of Christ, digging ripping peeling my own.

I wonder when I first stopped dropping the shards to the floor and began slipping them into my mouth instead, so my skin and Jesus's could be digested together.

I remember the discomfort of the sign of peace, OCD switching from my own hands to the hands of others and the unsanitary touch of my bleeding thumbs on theirs.

That's when I cultivated the half-nod-half-smile and tried to dodge their hands. I started to pine after romantic notions of polite curtsies and bows, no touching allowed.

No touching others with my unsanitary hands in the Sanctuary.

My brother dubbed it the "Franken-thumb" and when he saw me start to pick he would grab it and he'd hold it tightly during the homily, as the priest spoke of the ills of abortion, contraception, impurity.

I think he was trying to help, but the shame that flowed from his disapproving look and the death grip keeping my thumb from my lips were both entirely—unhelpful.

And you cannot fidget with the anxiety, panic, terror when you've only got one hand free. It just doesn't work that way.

It's more than 10 years since I started self-cannibalizing the flesh from my cuticles, the joints and pads of my thumbs and forefingers.

My fingers are still torn, and my thumb throbs dully as I write this.

I had to give up piano and violin for it. Neither was fun to play with bleeding, throbbing fingers.

I don't talk about it much. I'm not really interested in hearing the distrust of people who would consider me a freak, in seeing their pitying, grossed-out faces.

And I'm certainly not supposed to admit that I don't want to stop it. I don't want to heal.

Because then where would the anger and the fear go? Would they build and build in my body until I implode, holes torn through my stomach, nothing left of the fabric that once held me whole?

Odd. It's been 10 years now. I no longer consume Christ's Flesh as I did when I started. But I still tear and chew my own.

If he is in me, and I in him, does it count? Does my flesh become Eucharist?

No. I suppose the still-good-catholics would tell you, his life died in me when I stopped eating him.

So I'm stuck with eating just me.

Rose Menyon Heflin

The Atheist at Communion: A Sijo Sequence

It's a compulsion. Even though she stopped believing as a child,
she's still there like clockwork in that very last pew each Sabbath,
always giving generously, despite never shaking hands.

She holds her hymnal silently, stiffly, steadfastly refusing
to sing along, her muttered amens unheard under her breath
as, with a shake of her head, she declines communion again.

She is both the last to enter and the first to leave every week.
Alternately the subject of gossip and easily missed,
she is, nonetheless, the most consistent of parishioners.

She tries to stop, to avoid that old, familiar skirt and blouse,
but Sunday comes and she can't help herself, can't stop that great urge
traipsing up her spine and through her marrow, scratching a whisper,

similar to nails on a chalkboard - deeply excruciating -
not unlike the guilt she feels when she arrives, Bible in hand,
knowing if there were a Hell for atheists, this would be it.

Elizabeth Gade
Madonna Of The Morgue

Today my body asked me, when are you coming back home to me, can you open the door inside my ribcage and step back inside. Today my body asked me when will embodiment stop feeling like a body bag zipped tight against my torso. The throat chakra collapses on itself every time it hears the metal teeth of your zipper. This is the implosion of a star consuming itself. A vacuum where I used to reside. This body isn't a home, it's a haunting. Eyes blacked out and filled with your ghosts. Today my body asked me to come out of the basement and into the light, hips graveyard full and swinging.

Jane Medved

Skin Is Not Light

I will scratch down
to the light

and let it out again.

Scales of bark. Even a garden
snake can leave itself

behind.

      Flat kingdom of itching.

Light bleeds everywhere
anywhere. Welcome the dark,

close up the palace

of the heart and let the liver
harden, and be crowned.

      Lie flat and breathe.

Think of dew. Don't touch.

The veins are rising

from their paper valleys
a blister hatches.

      Take it back.

This pale palette
flanked by heel and palm

worn out, uncertain fence.

Let me slither it off.
I am already halfway there.

Poet Biographies

Elizabeth Johnston Ambrose
"The Ten Commandments of Loving a Recovering Evangelical"
Elizabeth Johnston Ambrose's fiction, poetry, plays, and literary nonfiction appear in *The Atlantic*, *McSweeney's*, *Room*, *Mom Egg Review*, *Rattle*, *Women Studies Quarterly*, and *Feminist Formations*, among others. She is the author of two chapbooks: *Wild Things*, (Main Street Rag, 2021) and *Imago, Dei* (winner of the Rattle Chapbook Poetry Prize, 2022). Coordinator of the Creative Writing Program at Monroe Community College and co-founder of the Rochester-based writing group Straw Mat Writers, she also facilitates a writing group for breast cancer survivors. She lives in Rochester, NY with her partner, daughters, and rescue animals. Find her at www.elizabethjohnstonambrose.com.

Bibi B.
"Parika" and "Durand Scarf"
Bibi is an ethnically Hazara artist and author, currently based in Metro Vancouver. She uses multiple mediums of art to explore the intersections of her identity and make sense of her place in the world. Bibi's piece "Lilt," was shortlisted for the Wabash Non-Fiction Prize, and published in Sycamore Review, issue 29.1.

Virginia Barrett
"Sunset IX"
Virginia Barrett is a poet, writer, artist, editor, and educator. She earned her MFA in Writing from the University of San Francisco where she was poetry editor of *Switchback*. Her six books of poetry include *Between Looking* (Finishing Line Press, 2019) and *Crossing Haight—San Francisco poems* (Jambu Press, 2018). Her prose has appeared in *The Writer's Chronicle*, *The Raven's Perch*, *Awakenings* and elsewhere. Lead designer for *Light on the Walls of Life—a tribute anthology to Lawrence Ferlinghetti* (Jambu Press, 2022), she is also the editor of four anthologies including *RED: a Hue Are You* anthology (Jambu Press, 2023). She has taught poetry, creative writing,

and visual art throughout the San Francisco Bay Area for over two decades, including in the MFA in Writing program at the University of San Francisco. www.virginiabarrett.com

Alex Baskin
"where god is called the Name"
Alex Baskin is a graduate of Harvard Divinity School. Rooted in over a decade of Buddhist practice and his upbringing in an orthodox Jewish family and community, he works as an interfaith hospital chaplain. His poetry appears in *Gulf Coast*, *Lucky Jefferson*, poetry.onl, *Redivider*, and elsewhere. He has an essay in *Refuge in the Storm: Buddhist Voices in Crisis Care* (North Atlantic Books, 2023.) Originally from New Jersey, he lives in Massachusetts.

Tara Campbell
"The prophecy unswaddled" and "Vessels of the State"
Tara Campbell is a writer, teacher, Kimbilio Fellow, fiction co-editor at Barrelhouse, and graduate of American University's MFA in Creative Writing. She teaches creative writing at venues such as American University, Johns Hopkins University, Clarion West, The Writer's Center, Hugo House, and the National Gallery of Art. She's the author of a novel, two hybrid collections of poetry and prose, and two short story collections from feminist sci-fi publisher Aqueduct Press. Her sixth book, featuring sentient gargoyles in the 22nd century American West, is forthcoming from Santa Fe Writers Project (SFWP) in Fall 2024. Find her at www.taracampbell.com

Emmie Christie
"How Do I Tell You"
Emmie Christie has been published in *Daily Science Fiction*, *Infinite Worlds Magazine*, and *Flash Fiction Online*. She graduated from the Odyssey Writing Workshop in 2013.

Kira Coleman
"Uninvited and Without a Recommend"
Kira Coleman graduated from Fordham University in English and Creative

Writing in 2021. She believes firmly that if you have something important to say, you have to say it, which is why she is a poet.

Dick Croy
"Prayer"
Dick Croy is a screenwriter, novelist and playwright. Writer and director of *The Fourth Dimension*, a documentary series of seven 60-minute television specials on the paranormal. His novel *The River Jordan*, co-authored with the late Henry Burke, was a book-of-the-year nominee. *Fugitive Slave,* their contemporary drama portraying the historical spirit of the Underground Railroad, is both an award-winning screenplay and a stage play which has received readings by the Classical Theatre of Harlem and other theater companies.

Allen Darwish
"Canon"
Allen Darwish is a middle-aged native Midwesterner, half Arab, half Celt, and all Crazy, future attorney, and all-around nerd. He's been writing poetry since high school; it used to be one of his main hobbies, and although it waned during my college and law school years, he's finally getting back into it.

Sheila Dietz
"Parking Lot Paradise"
Sheila Dietz (has also published as Sheila Bonenberger) is a "third culture kid" who grew up in the Netherlands and attended a Dutch school. The Dutch are known to be very direct (known as bespreekbarheid) which has influenced the tone of her work. She has taught as an adjunct in the English Department at Albertus Magnus College, where she received her BA, and at Southern Connecticut State University, where she received an MLS and taught for one year full-time in the English Department. She also received an MFA in Poetry from Vermont College. Sheila worked as a librarian at the New Haven Free Public Library retiring as Head of Reference Services in 2017. She is also the co-founder of the Salt and Pepper Gospel Singers (from New Haven, CT), which is reflected in her poems which are often,

though not always, spiritual in nature. Her poems have appeared in *The American Poetry Review*, *The Antioch Review*, *Beloit Poetry Journal*, *Crazyhorse*, *Denver Quarterly* and *The Massachusetts Review*, among others.

Elizabeth Gade
"Madonna of the Morgue"
Elizabeth Gade is a rural Minnesota based bisexual poet and human trafficking survivor. Writing is her radical way to connect with fellow survivors. Her poems have been published in *View Magazine, The Elevation Review, 300 Days Of Sun, Exist Otherwise* & more. Her self-published debut poetry collection *Fawn and Freeze* & poetry workbook *Survived To Write* is available on Amazon. Elizabeth created *LEO Literary Journal*, an online journal dedicated to women writers affected by incarceration, addiction and/or domestic violence. (www.LeoLiteraryJournal.Weebly.com) She is creator of Survived To Write, a survivor led writing circle for human trafficking survivors. Connect with her on Instagram @ElizabethGadeThePoet and @SurvivedToWrite

Elliot Gale
"The Life Cycle of the Transsexual"
Elliot Gale (he/they) is a trans artist and poet working in Massachusetts, USA. Much of his work, regardless of medium, directly addresses queerness, especially as it relates to personal identity and familial dynamics. He considers everything he creates to be inherently queer because of the nature of his handiwork. Their poetry is heavily free-verse and they enjoy experimenting with indentation, tense, and italicization.

Kristin Gifford
"Viriditas"
Kristin Gifford lives in Minneapolis where she writes at the crossroads of spirituality, motherhood, nature, and feminism. She is completing her first poetry collection with the Loft Literary Center's Poetry Apprenticeship and has been published in *Sojourners, Heimat Review, Kakalak, 3Elements,* and other journals.

Rose Menyon Heflin
"The Atheist at Communion"
Originally from rural, southern Kentucky, Rose Menyon Heflin is a poet, writer, and visual artist living in Madison, Wisconsin. She has had over 200 poems published in journals, magazines, and anthologies spanning five continents, and her poetry has won multiple awards. Additionally, one of her poems was choreographed and performed by a dance troupe, and she had a creative nonfiction piece featured in the Chazen Museum of Art's *Companion Species* exhibit. Among other venues, her poetry has been published in *After . . . , Deep South Magazine, Fahmidan Journal, Fathom Magazine, Fiery Scribe Review Magazine, Isotrope, Of Rust and Glass, Red Door Magazine, The Remnant Archive, Salamander Ink Magazine, San Antonio Review,*. An OCD sufferer since childhood, she strongly prefers hugging trees instead of people.

Shannon King
"Good Catholic Girl" and "Recovering Devout"
Shannon King is an artist, writer and independent scholar. She is an American-Canadian with roots on the East Coast. She received a BA in English and Art from the University of Toronto in 2022. She has recently had her poetry/art published online in *The 5-7-5 Journal, #Ranger, The TypeScript Journal, Slate, Bombuss Press, Technophilia: A Transhumanist Zine, STATIC ZINE,* and in *Curated by Covid: A Digital Gallery.* She has had poems featured in Florida Roots Press's recent anthology *Coming of Age in Florida.* Her artwork has been shown at Rochester Contemporary Art Center, University of Western, Visual Arts Mississauga, Joshua Creek Heritage Art Centre, and Gallery 1313.

Neethu Krishnan
"Her body as a receptacle for a Devi"
Neethu Krishnan is a writer based in Mumbai, India. She holds an MA in English and an M.Sc. in Microbiology, and writes between genres at the moment. Her works have appeared in over twenty-five international literary venues so far including *The Spectacle, Fu Review, The Saltbush Review,* and elsewhere. She is a Best of the Net poetry nominee and recipient of *Bacopa Literary Review*'s Creative Nonfiction Award. You can find her @neethu.krishnan on Instagram.

Stephanie Krist
"Yours No More"
Stephanie is a photographer, poet and aspiring children's book author. She graduated from Syracuse University with a BFA and lives outside of Worcester, MA with her husband and 5 year old son.

Angela Martz
"Prayer Circle, 1998"
By day, Angela Martz works in finance. Taking over twenty years of experience living in Mennonite and Evangelical circles, she strives to share her experiences with religion. She has a passion for platforming untold stories and emerging voices.

Jane Medved
"Skin Is Not Light"
Jane Medved is the author of *Deep Calls To Deep* (winner of the Many Voices Project, New Rivers Press) and the chapbook *Olam, Shana, Nefesh* (Finishing Line Press). Recent work has appeared or is forthcoming in *ONE ART: A Journal of Poetry, Literary Mama, Ruminate, The North American Review* and *The Contemporary Jewish Poetry Anthology* (Greentower Press 2023). Her awards include winner of the 2021 RHINO translation prize and the 2021 Janet B. McCabe Poetry Prize – Honorable Mention. Her translations of Hebrew poetry can be seen in *Hala, Hayden's Ferry Review* and *Copper Nickel*. She is the poetry editor of *The Ilanot Review*, and a visiting lecturer in the Graduate Creative Writing Program at Bar Ilan University, Tel Aviv.

Devon Miller-Duggan
"Prayer against Insomnia"
Devon Miller-Duggan has published poems in *The Antioch Review, Massachusetts Review*, and *Spillway*. She teaches at the University of Delaware. Her books include *Pinning the Bird to the Wall* (Tres Chicas Books, 2008), *Alphabet Year*, (Wipf & Stock, 2017), *The Slow Salute*, Lithic Press Chapbook Competition Winner, 2018).

Colleen Mitchell
"New Names"
Colleen Mitchell is a poet and author who shares the story of her life's journey through words. She is Louisiana born and bred, called Costa Rica home for six years, and now finds herself laying down roots in Fort Wayne, Indiana while she watches her five children grow into adults. She is passionate about the importance of story-telling, championing other women, and watching the moon grow full.

Hera Naguib
"Lessons from the Qari"
Hera Naguib holds a doctorate in creative writing from Florida State University, focusing on global and transnational poetry. Winner of the 2023 John Mackay Shaw Academy of American Poets Award and the 2022 *Quarterly West* Poetry Prize selected by Sally Wen Mao, her work has been published or is forthcoming in *Poetry Northwest, TriQuarterly,* The Academy of American Poets, *New England Review, The Cincinnati Review, Wasafiri, World Literature Today* and elsewhere. Her poetry manuscript, *Atlas of Disquiet*, was a finalist for the 2023 for the Brittingham and Felix Pollak Prizes in Poetry by the University of Wisconsin Press. Naguib has received support from VIDA: Women in Literary Arts and the Fulbright Program. She has led many writing workshops as an instructor at Florida State University, Forman Christian College University, Kinnaird College for Women, and Beaconhouse National University. Most recently, she served as seminar leader for "Poetry of Place," a poetry workshop session for young writers offered by the University of Iowa's International Writing Program.

Sumit Parikh
"Prayer Room"
Dr. Sumit Parikh is an emerging poet based in Cleveland, OH. His work has previously been featured in *Intima, a journal of Narrative Medicine.* Some of his work can be seen at his site sumitspoetry.com. He has participated in a writing mentorship and workshops with Brian Evans-Jones, who is a Poet Laureate of Hampshire, UK, and winner of the Maureen Egen Writers Exchange Award from *Poets & Writers*. Sumit is a pediatric neurologist at the Cleveland Clinic and graduated with honors in English from Case Western Reserve University.

Holly Payne-Strange
"Devotional Dinners"
Holly Payne-Strange's (she/her) is a published novelist, poet and podcast creator. Her writing has been described as "genuinely captivating" by *LA Weekly* and " profound and sincerely engaging" by *USA Today*. She was also a writer for *Fireside Mystery Theater*, which *The New York Times* called "One of the top ten podcasts to bring drama into your home". Her next novel, *All Of Us Alone*, will be a recommended read for Women Writers, Women's Books in December 2023. Her poetry has been published by various groups including *Curating Athena*, *Door Is A Jar* magazine, *In Parenthesis*, *Rising Sun Productions*, *Dipity Lit Magazine*, and will soon be featured in *Academy Heart*, among others.

Bethany W. Pope
"Speaking in Tongues"
Bethany W. Pope has won many literary awards and published several novels and collections of poetry. Nicholas Lezard, writing for *The Guardian*, described Bethany's latest book as 'poetry as salvation'......'This harrowing collection drawn from a youth spent in an orphanage delights in language as a place of private escape.' Bethany currently lives and works in China.

Trystan Popish
"Pedicure"
Trystan Popish (she/her) is a disabled poet from Colorado. In her work, Trystan plays with sound and internal rhymes, bringing a sonic levity to explorations of mental health, disability, family trauma, grief, survival, and religion. She is currently an editor for Twenty Bellows, and her work appears in *The Ekphrastic Review*, *Open Minds Quarterly*, and *Santa Fe Writers Project Quarterly*. Trystan lives with her husband, their brand new baby, type I diabetes, depression, and two dogs.

David E. Poston
"The Word"
David E. Poston is the author of two award-winning poetry chapbooks and the full-length collection *Slow of Study*. His poetry and fiction have appeared in *Atlanta Review*, *Broad River Review*, *Ibbetson Street*, *The MacGuffin*, and *Windhover*, among others. He is a co-editor of *Kakalak*.

Melinda Robinson
"The Flesh and the Devil"
Melinda is a reprobate pagan who left Catholicism to pursue worldly pleasures -- an altar strewn with succulents and Tarot, warm bodies curled in nests of blanket, and pages peppered with the just-right dirty words. She also writes poetry and studies philosophy.

David Ruekberg
"When God Visits Me"
David Ruekberg (MFA, Warren Wilson) is a poet, teacher, and climate activist in Rochester, NY. Poems have appeared in *Barrow Street, Borderlands, Cimarron Review, Lake Effect*, and elsewhere. His books include *Where Is the River Called Pishon?* (Kelsay Books, 2018) and *Hour of the Green Light* (FutureCycle Press, 2021). https://poetry.ruekberg.com.

Lynne Sargent
"A Priestess' Carvings"
Lynne Sargent is a writer, aerialist, and holds a Ph.D in Applied Philosophy. They are the poetry editor at *Utopia Science Fiction* magazine. Their work has been nominated for Rhysling, Elgin, and Aurora Awards, and has appeared in venues such as Augur Magazine, Strange Horizons, and Daily Science Fiction. Their work has also been supported through the Ontario Arts Council. To find out more visit them at scribbledshadows.wordpress.com.

P. Ashley Smith
"blame the dress"
P. Ashley Smith is an author, artist, and educator whose poetry follows the rabbit trails of a fascination with obscure knowledge, the natural world, and spirituality. She draws from the experiences of a fundamentalist childhood, several years spent in the slums of Rio de Janeiro, two decades of chronic illness, and an insatiable curiosity. Her training as a classical musician informs her choice of words and rhythms in both poetry and prose.

J. J. Steinfeld
"Ending Music of the Disoriented Soul"
Canadian poet, fiction writer, and playwright J. J. Steinfeld lives on Prince Edward Island, where he is patiently waiting for Godot's arrival and a phone call from Kafka. While waiting, he has published 24 books, including *An Unauthorized Biography of Being* (Stories, Ekstasis Editions, 2016), *Absurdity, Woe Is Me, Glory Be* (Poetry, Guernica Editions, 2017), *A Visit to the Kafka Café* (Poetry, Ekstasis Editions, 2018), *Gregor Samsa Was Never in The Beatles* (Stories, Ekstasis Editions, 2019), *Morning Bafflement and Timeless Puzzlement* (Poetry, Ekstasis Editions, 2020), *Somewhat Absurd, Somehow Existential* (Poetry, Guernica Editions, 2021), *Acting on the Island* (Stories, Pottersfield Press, 2022), and *As You Continue to Wait* (Poetry, Ekstasis Editions, 2022).

Charisse Stephens
"Transfiguration"
Charisse Stephens is a poet and teacher with a deep fascination for science, religion, history, and language. She grew up in the flatlands of northwest Ohio but always considered the mountains home, and she now lives in Salt Lake City with her partner, two kids, and dog Polly.

Marie Thomas
"Skin"
Marie Thomas is a sometimes poet living in the Ohio Valley wasteland just outside of Pittsburgh, PA. Her work has been published by *US Catholic*, the *Ethel Zine*, the *Bureau of Complaint*, and *Apparition Lit*, which nominated her poem "Apples in Hell" for the Pushcart Prize.

Madina Tuhbatullina
"Tender Primates III"
Madina is an international student from Turkmenistan, receiving a Creative Writing MFA degree at the University of Nevada, Las Vegas. Madina's poetry has been published or is forthcoming in *New Note Poetry, PubLab, great weather for MEDIA*'s anthology and elsewhere. Madina is an alumna of the Los Angeles Review of Books Publishing Workshop and Tupelo Press Manuscript Workshop.

Bernardo Villela
"A(scent)"
Bernardo Villela has short fiction included in periodicals such as *LatineLit*, *Penumbra Online* and *Horror Tree* and in anthologies such as *We Deserve to Exist, Enchanted Entrapments* and *There's More of Us Than You Know*. He's had original poetry published by *Phantom Kangaroo, Straylight*, and Raven's *Quoth Press* and translation published by *AzonaL and Red Fern Review*. You can find some of his other works here: https://linktr.ee/bernardovillela.

Melanie Weldon-Soiset
"Bound for Foxe's Book?"
Melanie Weldon-Soiset has poetry in *Clerestory, Sunlight Press, Tipton Poetry Journal*, and others. A 2022 Washington Writers' Publishing House contest winner, Melanie is a #ChurchToo survivor, former pastor, and Poetry Editor at *Geez* Magazine. Find her in real life biking on DC greenways. Find her online (including her poetry and prayer newsletter) at melanieweldonsoiset.com (IG: @MelanieWelSoi).

LaDonna Witmer
"Rubies / Proverbs 31:10"
LaDonna Witmer grew up in a Midwest farm town in a fundamentalist Baptist sect. She has been writing her way out for most of her life. She has published three books of poetry: *Shedding the Angel Skin* (2000), *The Secrets of Falling* (2007), and *New Hymns* (2019). In addition to writing a memoir about her fundamentalist upbringing, LaDonna regularly produces essays at wordsbyladonna.substack.com about her life in Palmela, Portugal.

Isabel Yacura
"spagyria of the liturgy"
Isabel Yacura is a writer and editor in Brooklyn, New York. She has been featured in *Kelp Journal, Zoetic Press, National Flash Fiction Day Anthology*, and other publications. She's currently represented by Haley Casey at CMA Literary, and can be found @isabelyacura on Twitter.

Acknowledgments

"The Ten Commandments of Loving a Recovering Evangelical" by Elizabeth Johnston Ambrose was first published in *Imago, Dei* (Rattle Magazine, Spring 2022) as the winner of their 2021 chapbook contest.

"Sunset IX [The Haight with Heaney]" by Virginia Barrett was first published in *Crossing Haight—San Francisco poems* (Jambu Press, 2019).

"where god is called the Name" by Alex Baskin was first published in *Lucky Jefferson*.

"The prophecy unswaddled" by Tara Campbell was first published by *HAD* (February 2023).

"Vessels of the State" by Tara Campbell was first published in *Poets Reading the News* (May 2019) and in *Political AF: A Rage Collection* (Unlikely Books, August 2020).

"The Atheist at Communion" by Rose Menyon Heflin was first published in *Global Poetry Consortium Mentor Anthology* (2022) and *Fathom Magazine*, (Issue 50, September 2022).

"Lessons from the Qari" by Hera Naguib was first published in *Gulf Coast* as "Rendezvous."

"THE WORD" by David E. Poston was first published in *Slow of Study* (Main Street Rag Publishing, 2015).

"When God Visits Me" by David Ruekberg was first published in *Hour of the Green Light* (FutureCycle Press, 2021).

"Ending Music of the Disoriented Soul" was first published in *Absurdity, Woe Is Me, Glory Be* (Guernica Editions, 2017) by J. J. Steinfeld.

www.ingramcontent.com/pod-product-compliance
Lightning Source LLC
LaVergne TN
LVHW041635070426
835507LV00008B/632